the wedding

**Paul Atterbury
and Hilary Kay**

the wedding

D&C
David and Charles

A DAVID & CHARLES BOOK
Copyright © David & Charles Limited 2005

David & Charles is an F+W Publications Inc. company
4700 East Galbraith Road
Cincinnati, OH 45236

First published in the US in 2005
First published in the UK in 2006

Text copyright © Paul Atterbury and Hilary Kay 2005

Paul Atterbury and Hilary Kay have asserted their right to be identified as authors
of this work in accordance with the Copyright, Designs and Patents Act, 1988.

A catalogue record for this book is available from the British Library.

ISBN-13: 978-0-7153-2216-1
ISBN-10: 0-7153-2216-8

Printed in China by R R Donnelly
for David & Charles
Brunel House   Newton Abbot   Devon

Commissioning Editor   Mic Cady
Desk Editor   Ame Verso
Project Editor   Susan Gordon
Art Editor   Prudence Rogers
Production Controller   Roslyn Napper

Visit our website at www.davidandcharles.co.uk

David & Charles books are available from all good bookshops; alternatively you can contact
our Orderline on 0870 9908222 or write to us at FREEPOST EX2 110, D&C Direct, Newton Abbot,
TQ12 4ZZ (no stamp required UK mainland); US customers call 800-289-0963 and Canadian
customers call 800-840-5220.

Introduction

This book is a celebration of the wedding through pictures from the earliest days of photography to the present day.

Western society has changed beyond recognition over the last 150 years, but there are some constants. The wedding is one of these. Whether hemlines are up or down, whether in a church, a synagogue, a register office or on a beach, the rituals remain the same.

The selected images of largely anonymous people capture the formality and the fun of the occasion. Affection between the bride and groom is recorded or found to be absent. The groom's mother looks disapprovingly at her new daughter-in-law, whether the photograph was taken in the 1890s or the 1980s.

The wedding of the Prince of Wales in 1863 was the first important royal wedding

to be recorded in a photograph. By the end of Victoria's reign the wedding photograph was established as the way in which every marriage should be commemorated.

The unwieldiness of a Victorian photographer's technical equipment meant that wedding couples were often photographed in the studio. In the early days subjects had to remain motionless for minutes on end, which may explain the lack of expression on the faces of these Victorian brides and grooms.

With the popularity of photography as a hobby in the Edwardian period, wedding photographs were no longer the sole territory of the professional. In the 1920s and 30s cameras became more portable, and a more informal style of wedding photograph became fashionable, inspired by society wedding pictures published in the newspapers.

Photographs of weddings in wartime are particularly poignant. Hastily arranged marriages are recorded in amateur snapshots – snapshots all too often destined to become the last trace of a loved one.

Basic, mass-market cameras introduced in the 1960s simplified the art of photography. Today video, mobile phone and disposable cameras are all present at weddings, and the resulting candid snapshots create an immediacy that brings the celebration to life.

The great survivor over the decades is the professional wedding photographer. For all our sophistication in this digital age, wedding parties are still obliged to stand about while the groups are posed. The wedding photo is alive and well, and remains the accepted way of recording a marriage.

9

Victorian

The wedding of Queen Victoria and Prince Albert on 10 February 1840 was greeted with great enthusiasm by the British public. Acres of publicity, masses of commemorative wares and plenty of discussion about the Queen's dress established a pattern followed by all subsequent royal weddings.

Drawings of the occasion appeared in papers and magazines, but photography was still in its infancy. The next great royal wedding in Britain was in 1863, when Edward, Prince of Wales, married Princess Alexandra of Denmark. This time cameras were present, as shown by this famous image. The dress, silver tissue decorated with Honiton lace and trimmed with chains of orange blossom and myrtle, was a sensation and versions of it were soon to be seen at weddings all over the country.

The influence of the royal family was not limited to dresses. Victoria's reign was marked by a sequence of well-publicized royal and aristocratic weddings, and thus was born the tradition of the wedding as the great moment of family celebration and extravagance, particularly among the emergent middle classes. The special wedding dress, in symbolic white or cream, became the focal point of these occasions, but was by no means universal. Many poorer women simply put on their best dress and the groom borrowed a suit.

Similar things were happening in the USA, particularly as society became more stable after the Civil War. By the 1880s photographers were documenting the true diversity of the country's culture and society, from the families of wealthy industrialists to poor farm workers, factory hands and former slaves. In between were the celebrities, entertainers, politicians, artists and others, whose weddings were promoted across the country.

Victorian

⟵indian army special

Service in India was a common British experience from the 1860s and many came home to seek a wife able to fulfil the demands of a society more British than Britain. This bride married an army officer in Simla in 1893. Elegant dresses, splendid uniforms and lovely flowers mark the event.

Mr & Mrs Tom Thumb

The marriage of Charles Stratton and Lavinia Warren in 1863 was a sensation. The world's first celebrity wedding, it was attended by 2,000 guests. Stratton, known since the age of 11 as General Tom Thumb, was famous throughout the world, thanks to his association with the circus impresario Barnum. Copies of this photograph, by Mathew B Brady, sold in huge numbers.

← borrowed suit

This 1870s bride wore her best dress and the groom a borrowed suit, judging by the length of the sleeves. Only the flowers, and the family history, tell us it is a wedding. This practice, common among poorer families, makes it hard to identify many Victorian images as wedding photographs.

↑ puff sleeves and patent leather

A smart wedding in Lincolnshire in the 1890s and the players are gathered in the marquee. Splendid beards and moustaches, fearsome hairstyles and a bride demurely casting her eyes to the ground set the scene. Two dashing young men, one looking after the family dog, repose as elegant bookends.

← midwest manners
The pose this couple has chosen makes a very formal statement about their marriage. Her dress is beautifully detailed; he looks smart. The Detroit photographer's French-style painted interior backdrop is just the latest thing.

a gentle passion →
The dress may be home-made but it reflects the fashions of the 1890s and is worn with confidence and elegance. The groom's jacket has perhaps seen better days but his bride is proud of him, and her hand rests lightly on his arm, showing off her new ring.

← a crinoline occasion

In this carefully composed group in front of a grand villa, all the women, including two little girls and the older ladies on the balcony, are in pale crinolines and lacy headdresses, an example of fashion conformity in 1860s Britain. Bride and groom look a bit uncertain, but it is too late for second thoughts.

harvest festival

In August 1869 a photographer took a wedding party into a cornfield and spent a long time arranging this scene. The formality of the crinolines, top hats and long jackets underlines the complexity of the composition. Two figures, probably servants, are informally dressed, one a young black boy.

Victorian

← best foot forward

This couple, photographed in Brighton in the 1890s in a gloriously detailed, painted studio interior, are clearly taking the marital journey seriously. She wears a smart dress with fitted jacket and puffed sleeves, he wears heavy, rustic trousers and a well-worn jacket – but his resolute expression shows he is determined to make the best of his new life.

Donovan

ST JAMES'S ST
BRIGHTON.

↞ a band of angels

In the early 1870s Hugh Mostyn married Ellen Duberly. Here he sits, withdrawn and straight-faced, probably overcome by so many strong and serious-looking women in matching white crinolines. The men are outnumbered, and nervous. Even his bride is keeping her distance. Things do not look promising.

↑ the stage is set

This photographer set himself a complex task. He has arranged the principals on the ground floor, and everyone else on the balcony, men evenly interspersed among the women, a group of children at one end, and in the centre, exactly above the unlikely-looking bride and groom, a child in a kilt.

17

Victorian

american dream →

In an 1890s studio in Mendota, Illinois, a young couple face up to the future. He is proud and forceful, his foot firmly on a low stool as if it were the head of the animal whose fur is spread out in front. She, a slender slip of a thing, stands wide-eyed and terrified. Her hat, like a stuffed exotic bird, rests on the table beside her.

CABINET · PORTRAIT
L. W. CLARK · MENDOTA, ILL.

← an informal approach

In front of a grand house somewhere in southern England in the 1870s, bridesmaids surround the best man in a flurry of lace. He looks directly at the camera. Forming the apex of a triangle, bride and groom look to one side. She holds his arm, comfortable with her new status.

⇧ fashion parade

In a glorious evocation of late-Victorian Britain, a party poses in front of
a grand house with a carpet-planted flowerbed in the foreground. It is a
panorama of fashion, with old ladies encased in black bombazine and taffeta,
and slender young girls in white dresses. A splendid couple, he in light suit
and hat, she in dynamic stripes, completely overshadows the bride and groom.

19

pretty little maids...

Bridesmaids are an enduring part of wedding tradition and, as ever, some will look gorgeous and some, forced into the kind and colour of dress they would not normally be seen dead in, look dreadful. They have clear duties, all wrapped up in making sure the bride is a princess for a day.

flower girl

This little poppet has remembered the flowers and the good-luck horseshoe. She has put on her cardigan in case it is a bit cold in the church, and her dress is looking lovely. She is desperate to do the right thing. But suddenly her responsibilities are about to overwhelm her.

best dress

Barely old enough to walk yet filled with pride, this little child is looking quite regal in her magnificent dress and hat. Her gloves wait on the chair. The late-Victorian photographer who captured this magic moment in South Wales deserved a medal.

H. Mortimer Allen

TENBY.

always the bridesmaid
Snapped on the sidewalk on their way to the church, these three show the spirit and style of 1950s America. Big dresses, big cars and a big billboard, promoting self-service shopping, set the scene. Across the road two passersby have stopped to watch it all.

← little ones
Children have always had supporting roles as bridesmaids and pageboys but here, in a French postcard of the Edwardian era, two children play the principal parts with panache, posing on a fine carpet.

five young fillies
The setting is a grand wedding in Edwardian England, and the five bridesmaids prepare for action. In their matching swagger-style dresses and striking hats, they could have stepped straight out of a painting by John Singer Sargent.

Edwardian

Britain went into mourning after the death of Queen Victoria in 1901, but with the coronation of Edward VII in 1902 the mood became more frivolous.

This new air of informality can be seen in this 1905 wedding photograph of Princess Margaret, bicycling enthusiast and granddaughter of Queen Victoria, and her groom, Prince Gustavus of Sweden. Her ivory satin dress was made in Ireland, covered with Carrickmacross lace in a design of Annunciation lilies, meadowsweet and shamrocks. The bridesmaids are dressed in blue satin and carry bouquets of simple daisies, symbolic of innocence and purity. Margaret was also known as 'Daisy'.

Women's lifestyles were beginning to change. Sports such as bicycling, roller-skating, golf and tennis became popular among women, and for the first time some went out to work as secretaries and clerks. As a result, women's clothes began to change radically. The neat and practical tailored suit became popular, and skirts that cleared the ground all round were worn with a blouse and fitted jacket. At last, corsets became more flexible and by 1910 women had relative freedom of movement.

Attitudes were shifting in America too. For the last 20 years the 'dollar princesses', heiresses from the fabulously wealthy railroad, real estate or mining families, had been marrying impoverished European aristocrats. Their weddings were marked by extraordinary excesses. After 1900 all this began to change, as Americans recoiled from extravagance and an anti-aristocratic backlash began to creep in. Weddings became much simpler affairs, embracing traditional American values of economy and hard work.

Edwardian

↓ suits you

The bride is dressed fashionably in a tailored suit and the groom in a lounge suit, showing that he is either a working- or middle-class man (others would have worn a morning or frock coat for a wedding). Both bride and groom have tight hold of their gloves – expensive accessories for their special day.

A Dog's Life

Pets often feature in wedding photographs. Generally they have a walk-on part as an extra to the main players, but occasionally they feature as supporting actors with such top-billing roles as bridesmaid, pageboy or best man. Today, on the Internet, you can purchase doggy gowns, tuxedos and formal wear in different sizes for the well-dressed canine wedding guest.

← happy pair

This working man and his bride are dressed
appropriately for their station in life, with no signs
of costly extravagance. Standing on a rug among
swags of cut paper flowers and flags and beneath
a handwritten 'God bless the happy pair' sign, the
couple have a fine start to their marriage.

↑ wedding à la mode

The church is under scaffolding, but this French
wedding party is making the best of things. The
groom wears a frock coat and the bride, in a tight-
hemmed dress, wears her veil modishly low on the
forehead. But, as ever, a child steals the show: look
at the little boy's outfit and his inappropriate hat.

Edwardian

Wishing you a happy Christmas.
From The Vicar and Mrs. Buss.
1911.

 ## top notch

Evidence that this is a well-heeled wedding can be seen in the bride's elaborate bouquet and embroidered gown and in the groom's top hat and frock coat. Gradually frock coats were superseded and by 1920 the morning coat was established as formal dress for monied gents.

court dress ➡

In aristocratic circles the wedding dress was worn by the bride at her first presentation at court after the wedding, a factor that influenced wedding fashions up to WWI. Attached to the shoulders of this dress is a long train, as was required to be worn at court.

← left a little

The Reverend Buss, surrounded by women of various ages, looks bemusedly at the photographer as his wedding portrait is arranged. One little bridesmaid in her Kate Greenaway-inspired frock squints at us. The unposed nature of the group makes it an interesting choice as the vicar's Christmas card.

↓ lounge lizards

At weddings in America and other countries, lounge suits were worn by men of all backgrounds. This artfully posed picture was taken in a studio in Accrington, Lancashire, England, so these sharp-suited chaps are probably from the working, rather than professional classes.

27

Edwardian

↞ **find the bride**

Two embroidered footstools pose at the front of this wedding photograph while the bride and groom are pushed to the rear, behind a host of attendants. The groom looks somewhat troubled as it dawns on him that his future role in this matriarchal group may be limited.

Tossing the Bouquet

In the late Middle Ages a wedding was followed by 'bedding the bride'. Guests accompanied the couple into their bedroom, helped them disrobe and snatched pieces of clothing for luck. As a measure of self-defence, brides resorted to throwing things to the guests instead. Today bouquets are tossed by the bride as the unmarried female guests jostle to be the lucky catcher — meaning that they will be the next bride.

HERE'S HAPPINESS

⬅ bride in black

The Faroes, an archipelago of 18 islands in the north Atlantic roughly midway between northern Scotland, western Norway and eastern Iceland, has a population of fewer than 50,000. At this Faroe Island wedding the bride follows a local tradition and wears a black dress for good luck.

⬆ no man's land

Men have been banished from this group of grim and determined matriarchs gathered in what looks like a prison exercise yard. The bride hovers timidly at the edge, beside her half-hidden bridesmaids. The younger women wear fashionable dresses with tiny waists and leg o'mutton sleeves.

29

↑ double trouble

Are the brides sisters, or are the grooms brothers? Either way, this heavily populated Edwardian double wedding looks like a milliner's shop window. The ladies' hats are wide-brimmed and artistically trimmed. The only male headgear to be seen is an unusual choice for a wedding, an embroidered smoking hat.

breathe in ➜

The bride standing stiffly beside her husband may have found it painful to sit. The tightly laced corsets of the 1900s featured a long piece of metal at the front, designed to dig into the groin if the woman did not arch her lower back. This created the fashionable S-shape figures of the day. The romantic Bo-Peep crooks held by the older bridesmaids could come in handy should the younger children become unruly.

autumn ➤ wedding

A proud day for the bride's father who is clad in his best suit and wears a smart eight-piece tweed cap. Dressed in an unpretentious high-waisted dress of embroidered cotton, the bride holds a bunch of chrysanthemums, which stand for those essential wifely qualities of cheerfulness and truth.

the funny side...

Wedding humour has been around for ages, and there are many postcards making fun of the matrimonial state. Perennially popular is the depiction of the groom as a victim, dragged reluctantly to the altar by a monstrous bride. Other themes include the bumpy road to true romance.

reluctant victim
This groom is very unhappy at the thought of life with the large and determined lady who has him firmly by the arm. The whole idea makes him sick. Or is it the drink (which probably got him into this spot in the first place)?

map of ➛
matrimony
There are several versions of this Edwardian joke about the long and uncertain journey to matrimonial bliss. This is a good one, posted in Cornwall in 1905. The journey begins at Bachelor Cove and the Spinster Isles and eventually, after many difficulties, reaches Cupid's Harbour, the town of Bliss and the Lake of Presents.

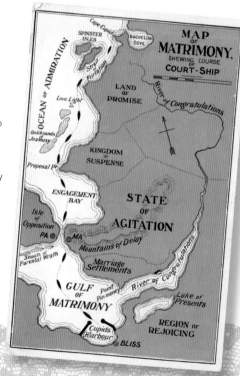

"UNSUSPECTING VICTIMS USED TO BE SACRIFICED AT THE ALTAR!"

"WE HAVEN'T ADVANCED MUCH SINCE THEN—

IT'S STILL HAPPENING—EVERY DAY!

sacrificial lamb

A large, dominant lady and a weak little man is a favourite theme for the British seaside postcard, that bastion of political incorrectness. Add matrimony and the reluctant groom to this brew, and the results are vulgar and entertaining.

"There was I waiting at the Church."

waiting at the church

Another popular theme is the abandoned bride, echoing the famous music hall song of that era. It is almost a counterpoint to the reluctant groom, showing that escape is possible. Sadly, this 1907 card seems to be the real thing, for the message from Dot says: 'waiting at the church so long, it is so disappointing.'

WWI

While the harsh reality of warfare was all too evident in northern France, on the home front it was largely life as usual. Marriages already planned took place, others were set in train. The major change since the Edwardian wedding was that photographs featured men in uniform. As the war progressed, everyone was drawn into the conflict. Conscription was introduced, and women began to play their part as nurses, drivers and factory girls. As the war took its toll, the optimism of the early years was soon replaced by a grim sense of resignation. The arrival of the dreaded telegram announcing the death of a loved one, and with it the huge sense of grief, became a common experience, shared by wives, fiancées and girlfriends all over Britain and across the colonies. A generation of women was destined to be widows or spinsters.

Despite this, the habit of marriage died hard. Men on leave continued to marry, driven by the desire to believe in some kind of future. In this photograph, taken early in the war, bride and groom lean towards each other and link arms, holding on to what little they have. Many of the women look worried, aware that the men in uniform are unlikely to return.

When peace finally returned, on 11 November 1918, there was a global sigh of relief. Normal life resumed. The survivors wanted to build themselves a stable future, with the conventional trappings of domestic life. There was a marriage explosion. Long engagements were finally consummated, and new relationships, often between wounded men and their nurses, offered a different kind of hope. So, in the immediate aftermath of the war, uniforms are still to be seen in wedding photographs.

↑ allons, mes enfants

Full of optimism, a French sailor stands with his new bride in the elaborate painted setting of a photographer's studio in Brest, Brittany. They are a handsome couple – he sports a fine moustache. They hold hands as they look at the camera with calm confidence and she, wearing a fashionable loosely fitted, straight dress, rests her hand on his shoulder, a rare indication of tenderness in photos of this era.

↞ peace at last

Poppy and Bertram married in 1919. Bertram, a senior army officer, is looking forward to a peacetime career after the rigours of the war. The little girl could well be Poppy's daughter. Perhaps the father was killed in action and her mother is making a new life for them both.

↑ lest we forget

A soldier from the Machine Gun Corps and his bride sit in a Hampshire garden during their wedding celebrations. He leans forward, uneasy and nervous, but she looks quietly confident. His best man, a Grenadier Guardsman, has dressed in his best uniform. It is a domestic scene, overlaid by the certainty of imminent return to service.

for whom the bell tolls ➡

The wedding was quickly arranged and the bride's outfit looks hastily assembled. In a few days the groom will return to the front. As a 2nd lieutenant in the infantry, he has only a slender chance of survival, and she knows that her likely fate is a few days' desperate happiness, months of loneliness, then the telegram and years of grief.

in sickness and in health

The bride cannot conceal her delight as she stands close to her handsome groom, a captain in a Scottish regiment. We know from other photographs in the album that he returned home wounded, but she cared for him and was able to restore him to health.

⟵ a domestic affair

A group has gathered in a fairly well-to-do house in Gloucestershire, probably in 1914, and presumably to celebrate a marriage. The groom, a lance corporal, appears confident and ready for anything. The dark-coloured dresses worn by his bride and most of the other women look so similar they could be a kind of uniform. Only the flowers and the hats suggest that it is a wedding photograph.

⟶ wartime romance

This carefully composed group has been photographed, like many others, in the back garden, amid the cabbages. The bride has a well-made, long dress with fine detailing and her groom is dressed formally, complete with top hat but in a suit made for a taller man. His mother, in elegant Edwardian-style silk dress, is evidently not too sure about her new daughter-in-law – but of course mothers never are. The groom seems to have escaped military service so far. Perhaps he is in a reserved occupation, or maybe his time will come with conscription.

beautiful blooms...

Whether it is just a few flowers gathered in the garden or a master florist's display of orchids, the bride's bouquet is an integral part of the ritual. Traditionally paid for by the groom, the bouquet is also an opportunity for the knowing bride to send a message through the time-honoured meanings of the flowers themselves.

size matters

Roses, ferns, ribbons and a horseshoe contribute to make this a jumbo-sized floral display for a 50s bride. Large bouquets were sometimes used as camouflage by brides whose burgeoning figures would otherwise show that they had experienced the joys of the honeymoon before the wedding!

in the pink

When we realize the meaning of the flowers this bride is holding, we see that, knowingly or not, she was practically writing a love poem. The pale pink roses stand for friendship, while the darker, more passionate pink variety symbolize love, grace, gentility and perfect happiness.

blooming marvellous

This Edwardian group is dominated by breathtaking hats and fabulous flowers. For decades it was customary for the bride to wear orange blossom in her hair or within her bouquet. This plant holds flowers and fruit on the same stem and is taken to symbolize marriage, fruitfulness and eternal love.

new look

These bridesmaids wear the wide skirts made popular by Dior's New Look of 1947, but their ribbon-trimmed posies of flowers in paper doilies are more reminiscent of Victorian weddings. The orchids in the bride's bouquet symbolize love, refinement and, in Chinese tradition, that she will bear many children!

1920s

After the horrors of World War I, the 1920s offered peace, prosperity and fun. The new decade saw a return of frivolity with jazz to dance to, cocktails to drink and films to see at the cinema. It was a good time to fall in love, and nothing could epitomize the optimism that marked the start of the decade better than a wedding!

However, women, and brides, had changed. Women had been playing a vital role during the war years, and the characteristics looked for in a bride were evolving. Significantly, the pre-publicity for a 1922 royal wedding between Princess Mary and Viscount Lascelles showed images of the princess in her VAD uniform nursing sick children.

No longer seen as a frail figure who must be protected by the groom, the bride was now regarded as a capable individual and a good companion.

Fashion of the 1920s reflected this. Women's hair was cut short and worn in a shingled style or a bob. Corsets were discarded and the look became more boyish with shorter dresses worn loose and low-waisted, minimizing the bust.

All these elements can be seen in this 1922 photograph. The bride, Marilyn Miller, one of the most beloved stage stars of the time, wears a gorgeous loose dress of lace and chiffon with a handkerchief hem, and a close-fitting, narrow-brimmed cloche hat.

Mary Pickford, the first international film pin-up, stands to the bride's right in a sleeveless dress with fine ribbon decoration. The groom is Jack Pickford, Mary's ne'er-do-well brother, wearing spats beneath his morning suit. Douglas Fairbanks, Mary's film star husband, is more up-to-the-minute with a smart waistcoat beneath his morning coat.

← new woman

This 1920s Parisian bride epitomizes a new breed of woman – a woman who smoked, drank and voted, listened to jazz, watched movies and chatted on the telephone. She wore make-up and went unchaperoned to parties, where she danced the 'Charleston' and the 'Black Bottom'.

natty hat

The groom may perhaps have borrowed his suit from a shorter man, but his hat shows up-to-the-minute fashion sense. Soft felt hats became popular for men in the 1920s. The trilby, which symbolized democracy and equality at this time, was often worn by men who moved in artistic or intellectual circles.

all bar one

Although bar shoes were first worn by adults in the 1880s, it was not until the 1920s, with shorter dress lengths, that they were really visible. They proved to be good at staying put during the more energetic dances of the day. Today they are referred to as 'Mary Janes' and are back in fashion.

⚓ prudent choice

This bride is neither the first nor the last to hold a large bridal bouquet in a strategic position to mask a spreading waistline. As costumes that will have to be worn on other occasions in the future, the dresses of coloured silk are a sound economic investment by the bride and her maid of honour.

A NEWLY MARRIED COUPLE LEAVING THE OLD BLACKSMITHS SHOP GRETNA GREEN AFTER THEIR WEDDING OVER THE FAMOUS ANVIL

Gretna Green

Gretna Green first became popular for weddings after a 1754 Act of Parliament decreed that, in England, the bride and groom must be over 21 to marry without parental consent. Scottish law, however, allowed couples to marry without parental consent from the age of 16. Since Gretna Green is just the Scottish side of the border, this village became the 'Marriage Mecca' for runaway English couples. The ceremony was often performed by one of the village blacksmiths, important and respected members of the community.

← wedding car

Innovative photographers sometimes made use of a luxurious car as an alternative to the painted backdrops and formal poses of the studio. Even if the wedding couple could not afford to arrive or leave in a real car, a credible illusion could be created for the wedding photograph album.

↓ meet the glums

Here bride and groom link arms in a fairly resigned sort of way, while the 25 friends and relatives, including several children, stare at the camera with barely a glimmer of a smile between them. The outlook for a frolicsome honeymoon and a fun-filled start to married life does not look optimistic.

↑ garden party

A joyful and relaxed family wedding group. The best man is standing on a wooden box so that he can be seen over the heads of the happy couple in front. The groom seems to be particularly keen for us to admire his striped socks, and we should not look too closely at what the child on the left is up to!

← wish you were here?

This hand-tinted, sepia image appears on one of the thousands of romantic postcards that were popular in the 1920s. The bride wears her veil fashionably low on the forehead, while her dewy-eyed beau offers a spray of white carnations, symbolic of innocence and pure love.

↑ showing some leg

Hems started to rise in the 1920s, first to above the ankle, then, between 1925 and 1927 to just below the knee. These drop-waisted dresses are made of soft, draping fabrics with handkerchief hems. Rayon stockings became popular after 1923, and were often worn rolled over a garter belt.

Solemn Vows

The words of the marriage ceremony are glorious, emotive and powerful, particularly in the traditional 17th-century version. Even modern versions retain much of the flavour and meaning. The moment when the vows are spoken in a crowded church is often unforgettable, the culmination of a ceremony steeped in ritual.

⇐ dutch hats and diadems

This bride is wearing a diadem headdress of artificial pearls – these became stylish for weddings in the late 1920s, as did dresses with hems longer at the back than at the front. The choice of hat for her little bridesmaid is also in the latest style, a bonnet in the form of a winged Dutch hat.

50

← class act

The simplicity of women's clothes in the 1920s made it look easy for a working-class girl to look like a rich girl on her big day. This bride, with her wreath of orange blossom and her spray of lilies, appears to be marrying a cad, who stands nonchalantly beside her, hand in his pocket.

↑ garden glory

By now it was acceptable for men to wear lounge suits to weddings, even in elevated social circles, but this groom has dressed more formally in frock coat and spats. He turns his attention to one of the bridesmaids, while his bride, with orange blossom circling her head, looks up at the photographer.

let them eat cake...

A traditional wedding cake is an architectural masterpiece, a multi-storey edifice intricately decorated with sugary encrustations. The tradition has its roots in Roman times when bread was crumbled over the bride as a fertility rite. Today the cake is still a key part of the wedding ritual, as rich in symbolism as it is in fruit. British weddings usually feature a dark fruit cake, which is often more of a symbol than a delicacy.

← food for thought

Rookie actor Lauren Bacall met established Hollywood superstar Humphrey Bogart in 1944 on the Warner Brothers' lot during the making of *To Have And Have Not*. She was 19, he was 44. The chemistry between the two was powerful, both on screen and off, and the following year they were married at writer Louis Bromfield's Ohio farm.

american traditions

In America, the dark fruit cake is associated with the groom and traditionally rests on top of the Bride' Cake, which is light in both colour and texture. The Bride's Cake is cut at the reception, and bride and groom feed each other with a mixture of affection and slapstick.

a potent symbol
Besides representing friendship, love, generosity, sweetness and fruitfulness, the wedding cake symbolizes the sharing of the hopes, dreams and hard work inherent in any marriage. The white icing represents purity, the tiers are for prosperity. The top tier of the cake is often preserved for the couple's first anniversary or for the baptism of their first child.

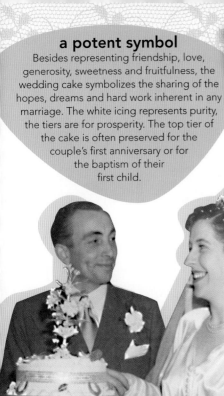

make a wish
The ritual of cutting the cake is one of the most unchanging elements in any wedding celebration. Once thought to symbolize the impending loss of the bride's virginity, it is the first task the couple undertakes jointly, as man and wife, and is underlined by the making of wishes.

each to his own
Not everyone wants the traditional tiered cake and today there are really no rules. Here, individual decorated cakes are arranged in layers beneath the traditionally iced top tier, decorated with bold gerbera.

1930s

The 1930s, more than any other decade, was influenced by film and the cinema. Hollywood movies, with their glamour and romance, were inspirational. Now every woman wanted to be a star on her wedding day.

Also on the scene was a new type of wedding photograph. Photographers were making use of the new smaller, lighter cameras to wander around the reception taking informal snaps. These candid photographs brought society weddings to life in a way the formal image could never do. They became hugely popular features in the newspapers and magazines, and encouraged other brides to emulate.

Weddings were now no longer home-made celebrations but packages that could be purchased. Professionals stepped in to take on the cooking, sewing and flowers, once the sole responsibility of the bride and her family, and department stores began to offer wedding services.

Illustrated here is the decade's most newsworthy wedding. It took place in France on 3 June 1937, when Edward, eldest son of King George V, married the twice-divorced Mrs Wallis Simpson of Baltimore. Wallis was a fashion icon of her day and wore a long, flowing dress of pale blue crêpe satin, by the American-born designer Mainbocher, and a hat trimmed with feathers. The groom wore a black morning suit. But this marriage cost Edward, who had succeeded his father as King Edward VIII, the throne. The British establishment would not allow Wallis to be queen, and Edward found it impossible to be king, in his own words, 'without the help and support of the woman I love'. He abdicated, and they spent the rest of their lives in exile.

1930s

⬅ akron anon

Akron, Ohio, is best known as the town where Alcoholics Anonymous was formed. This Akron wedding is very stylish, particularly the maid of honour in her 'Dolly Varden' hat. The bridesmaids appear to have swapped dresses just for fun.

⬅ net benefit

Standing in the front garden of a row of houses, this is obviously a happy group. The unsophisticated dresses are of fashionable soft, flowing fabrics with cinched waists. The only touches of glamour are the net headdresses that complete the bridesmaids' ensembles.

←victorious vicar

This couple are suitably dressed for a chilly autumn wedding. The bride's velvet ensemble is trimmed with fur at the neck and cuffs, and she clutches a splendid bouquet of late-flowering chrysanthemums. The groom, with his flamboyant buttonhole, is wrapped snugly in an overcoat and is keeping firm hold of his hat.

↑ sumptuous simplicity

An understated and, correspondingly, very smart wedding. Informally posed outside the church, the bride wears a bias-cut dress and holds a simple arrangement of arum lilies. The bridesmaids wear crocheted 'Juliet' caps and trendy fingerless gloves of fine knitted lace. The sweet peas they carry may provide a clue to the colour of their dresses.

⬆ hollywood heroine?

The influence of Hollywood is apparent, and the bride at this grey London wedding could have stepped straight from the pages of a movie magazine. She is luminous in her shimmering, bias-cut gown, which is tightly belted and features bizarre barnacle-like rosettes applied at the bust and hip.

Shotgun Wedding

This comic postcard dating from about 1920 shows the classic wife or death scene. The parson points, the groom stands abashed and the pregnant bride glances wistfully at her swollen belly. No doubt, just outside the frame, the bride's father is lurking with his shotgun loaded. Although in the Western world today there is little stigma in bearing a child out of wedlock, in many other cultures it is still regarded as scandalous.

L'AUVERGNE

Un Mariage en Auvergne
Las fauait Petchai d'avant lu Raipans

← well suited

Looking like a matinée idol with his brilliantined hair, this groom is a picture of fashionable tailoring in his suit of wide pinstripe. His bride wears a gown with a sweetheart neckline made of patterned lace over a satin underdress, the costume completed with a lace mob cap. The only discordant note in this idyllic scene is the inclusion of a drainpipe.

↓ dog days

A case of 'love me, love my dog'? Or perhaps the bride has found truth in the old adage 'the more I know about men, the more I love my dog'? There is no obvious groom and the assorted menfolk, drawn from a number of regiments including the Royal Artillery, toast the worried-looking bride with military precision.

Hat Heaven

Where would a wedding be without its handful of hideous hats? It is an aspect that transfixes the mothers of the bride and groom for months in advance and, more often than not, the result is millinery meltdown. This picture shows some exhilarating Edwardian headgear. One of the small girls has a Kate Greenaway-style poke bonnet, and the older women appear to have plundered flora and fauna for their hats: one is trimmed with a bird's wing, others with flowers and feathers.

↑ doorstep fashion

It is half hidden by the large bouquet of roses, but we can be sure the bride's dress, with its jolly printed design, handkerchief hemline and fashionable bias cut, will be worn many times after the wedding. The groom's spats and wing collar show that he is also a snappy dresser.

← lucky man

It was a royal bride, Princess Marina, who in 1934 first popularized the diadem as fashionable bridal wear. It is worn to full effect here by this beaming nymphet, who clutches her lucky horseshoe. This diadem is probably made from decorated wire rather than diamonds and pearls though.

↑ muffled muddle

The classic fashion blunder: the adult bridesmaids' dresses are the same style as the little girls'. No one looks happy with the result. And bad is made worse by the addition of muffs, which jar horribly with these short-sleeved summer dresses. The girls all wear identical crucifixes – presented by the groom?

Wedding Breakfast

Despite its name, traditionally the wedding breakfast was served at noon. It can be simple or extravagant. Actor Kate Winslet famously served her guests bangers and mash (sausages and mashed potatoes) to celebrate her 1998 marriage to James Threapleton.

⚜ naval nuptials

A naval officer with his bicorn under his arm seems to be standing to attention for this photograph. His bride wears a flowing gown of medieval influence and, to complete the minimalist look, adopts the fashion for an understated spray of arum lilies.

FRANK LINDER · MARRIED
THIS COUPLE AS IS — IN
STAGE · GARAGE

← ring of confidence

The groom sports a lucky-horseshoe buttonhole
and displays his wedding ring with aplomb. The
women wear dresses with gathers and flounces,
clearly inspired by earlier styles, but the soft
materials, the printed fabric for the bridesmaids'
dresses and their net hats are all up-to-the-minute.

↑ fares please

This couple just couldn't wait! Looking excited,
they balance on the running-board of a motor bus
in a garage en route from San Francisco to San
Jose. The wedding was conducted, perhaps in
more ways than one, by Frank Linder, who may be
the figure holding a book on the right.

63

lovely lingerie...

Silks, satins and lace have been winning combinations (in every sense of the word) over the decades. Brides are certain to choose special underwear for the wedding and honeymoon. It is a perfect opportunity for a little extravagance, helping her to feel confident and attractive on the big day.

bottom drawer

A Victorian bride began sewing her trousseau and linens as a child. She would bring to her new life at least eight nightdresses, eight drawers, eight chemises and eight corset-covers. Made from French nainsook, cambric and lawn, they were trimmed with ribbons and lace and bore the bride's initials.

↓ hourglass figure

Contemporary designers have revived the corset, which women were so relieved to have escaped from in the 1920s. Pop diva, Kylie, famously used one designed by specialist corset-maker Mr Pearl to reduce her already slim waist down to a reputed circumference of just 16 inches!

ravishing rayon ⟶
Artificial silk was invented in the 1850s, but commercial production did not start until the early 20th century. The name Rayon was first used in 1924, and it became the new must-have fabric. These two styles of plain chemise in satin and artificial silk appear in a bridal magazine from the 1930s.

wedding night ⟶
The wedding over, the final waltz danced, the last champagne flute emptied, the bouquet thrown, the confetti brushed from the collar and, finally, the wedding night has arrived. This 1960s blushing bride has changed into something more comfortable and looks a picture of coy temptation. Her seductive nightdress of silk chiffon is a confection of ribbon, bows and lace.

it's a pet!

Keystone
lingerie

perfect pet-icoat
With a nipped waist and wide skirts, this is the perfect foundation for a fashion-conscious bride of the 1950s. The advertisement features the ubiquitous poodle – a visual shorthand to indicate Parisian fashion and style.

65

1940s

The last years of the 1930s were overshadowed by the threat of war, and no one was surprised when Europe exploded in September 1939. At first, things in Britain did not change radically, even as the Nazis rampaged across Europe. Uniforms were everywhere, children were evacuated from city centres and the blackout was introduced, but there were no immediate shortages. People continued to get married. Indeed, the number of marriages increased as couples, faced by the prospect of enforced separation, rushed to make the most of whatever time they had together.

The reality of the war hit hard in 1940 with the fall of France, the Blitzkrieg on British cities, and the desperate implications of Britain standing alone in a conflict that seemed set to last for years. Rationing and self-sufficiency took over, underlined by slogans such as 'Make Do and Mend'. Though posed, this famous image reflects the spirit of the London blitz in 1940. The house is in ruins after a visit from the Luftwaffe but the theme is Carry On Regardless.

In a beleaguered Britain, the cinema offered a vital escape and Hollywood made sure there was plenty to watch. In the real world in Britain, weddings still took place, but were hastily arranged, a snatched moment in a couple of days' leave. Often the wedding dress was made from curtain fabric or was replaced by a borrowed dress. Men wore their uniforms. When peace returned in 1945, nothing changed in a Britain now locked into austerity. Rationing remained, and for most women the New Look was just a dream on a distant horizon. In America things were, as ever, very different, but for Britain the United States was indistinguishable from Hollywood.

a safe haven

It is September 1944, the end of the war is in sight and optimism is all around. The groom and his best man are in the Royal Navy Voluntary Reserve, and there is work still to be done. The bride's dress is cunningly made from lace and her bridesmaids' dresses from curtain net – all available without clothing coupons.

let's do it

The war is still young. Her dress is home-made and the style is 1930s but she has managed to get some satin. He is in the RAF and his prospects still seem rosy. They are delighted to be married but have chosen a strange place for the photograph, on rough ground below the old pigeon shed.

←boys in blue

A wartime wedding in Kent, and the bride is determined to make the most of whatever the future offers. Her groom and his best man are aircrew, perhaps Bomber Boys, living from day to day – though the medals suggest the groom has already had a busy war. The bride's dress is probably a borrowed 1930s number, while the girl on the left wears a classic 1940s two-piece.

↑ meanwhile…

In Hitler's Germany, a huge family affair is being recorded. It is probably 1939 or 1940 as there is one man in uniform. The photograph is very formal, and balanced, with the children, particularly the two with embroidered cushions, carefully posed. Most people look happy and the bride and groom seem to like each other. It is the calm before the storm.

austerity style

This picture underlines the reality of the wartime wedding. The groom and the bridesmaid wear battledress, the bride makes do with a plain two-piece and a jaunty hat. But they all look pretty cheerful. Best dressed are the couple on the left, he in a natty suit, she in her fox fur.

an american classic

The groom is dashing in uniform and the bride, with her amazing hair and lipstick, looks like Jane Russell. Against a draped backdrop, they adopt the classic American wedding pose, not touching and with the emphasis on the bride and her great sweep of very carefully managed dress.

the mexican way

Is the bride, perched on a stuffed donkey in a photographer's studio in Tijuana, having second thoughts? Or maybe it is just her dress that is worrying her? The groom is looking confident and his friends seem fairly relaxed about it all, especially the straw hats.

it's going to be ok

The group poses outside the church as the wind catches the dresses and brings it all to life. The bride is radiant, the handsome groom is happy and everyone else seems glad to be there. The war is probably over. They have come through. Somehow, someone has found plenty of fabric and it's all satin and lace.

← triumphant bride

This bride is delighted to have her man. He, a sergeant major in the Royal Army Service Corps, may be facing his biggest challenge of the war but he looks willing enough, even if his shoulders are drooping a bit. The group stands in a generous garden setting and, unusually, the vicar has joined the photograph.

▼ bedside manners

The setting is a military hospital in India, she is a nurse, he a junior doctor. She wears a pretty flowery dress, perhaps made from fabric bought in the market, he is in ordinary tropical kit. Clearly his commanding officer and her matron have given their blessing and have joined the party.

40s flair ↝

This bride is the picture of fashion with a pillbox hat at the correct jaunty angle, a bouclé jacket, and a coat with just the right amount of flare. He wears what looks like his demob suit. Arm-in-arm they face the future, at a time when life in Britain was far from easy.

↓ nice girls love a sailor

The bride tenderly links her arm through her groom's and they both put on a brave face for the photographer, although the longevity of any wartime marriage rested with the fates. Optimistically, the bride holds a bouquet that includes sprays of gypsophila, which in the language of flowers means everlasting love.

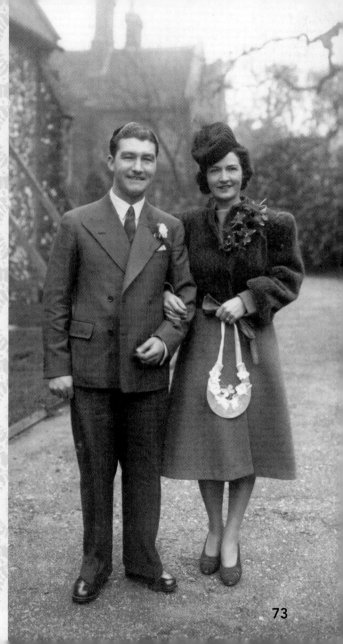

73

✎ a church family

Two clergymen, one an army chaplain, flank this group. The setting is a large garden somewhere in England, perhaps an old rectory, as parents of both bride and groom seem to be church people. The garden may well have supplied the bride's abundant flowers. The war is well advanced but there is probably plenty of fighting still to be done by the groom and his best man.

Wedding Presents

The presents ritual is well established. 'The list' dates back to Victorian days, and the gifts were often put on display at weddings. Presents are all part of the nest-building process, and for many brides are a highlight of the day. This 1930s bride appears much more excited by her lovely new sheets than by the man she is about to marry.

← it's all over

In November 1945 Les and Joy were married
in Handsworth, near Birmingham, England.
She has waited so long for him to come home.
Big hat, big bouquet, a lucky horseshoe and a
demob-style striped suit complete her picture,
while he stands to attention in his battledress.
The war is over, now for the peace.

↑ facing the future together

Peace has returned and everyone looks
cheerful. The impact of thrift, make do and
mend, and utility is very apparent, particularly
in the matching skirts on the left and the
bridesmaid's flowery number. The bride has
probably adapted something pre-war. The
small boy on the right has brought his camera.

getting ready...

The longed for day dawns, and it is an early start to make sure everything fits into place. Bridesmaids, the mother of the bride, the hairdresser all pull together to create their very own princess. Make-up, final adjustments to the dress, flowers are all part of the transformation, and all those little rituals must not be forgotten.

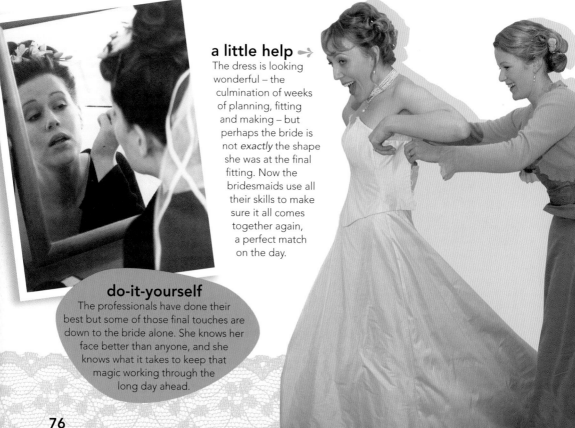

a little help →
The dress is looking wonderful – the culmination of weeks of planning, fitting and making – but perhaps the bride is not *exactly* the shape she was at the final fitting. Now the bridesmaids use all their skills to make sure it all comes together again, a perfect match on the day.

do-it-yourself
The professionals have done their best but some of those final touches are down to the bride alone. She knows her face better than anyone, and she knows what it takes to keep that magic working through the long day ahead.

calm before the storm ➙

Everything is ready and the bridesmaids have checked and double-checked. The bride is with the hairdresser, so there is a period of calm as the dress and the accessories await their moment. Soon all will be turmoil, drama and, ultimately, spectacle.

something borrowed

Everyone follows the old rituals. The chief bridesmaid slips on the garter, that hidden symbol of mystery that will later be removed and thrown to the guests. Many brides wear two, one to throw and the other to be removed by the groom in a more private moment after the celebrations.

1950s

This was the decade that saw the emergence of the first 'teenagers', who responded to their introduction to rock 'n' roll – Bill Haley's 'Rock Around the Clock', used in a movie soundtrack – by ripping up their cinema seats. But it was also the decade that saw the creation of *Playboy* magazine and the 'Barbie' doll, both of which said something else about the way women were regarded.

During the 1920s, 30s and 40s women had proved themselves capable and independent, but their hard-won freedom was put to one side as World War II came to an end. Women were encouraged to give up work to make sure that there were enough jobs for the returning soldiers, and wives were expected once again to focus on being the angel of the home.

Grand, formal wedding ceremonies came to be regarded as every girl's right for her special day. Brides-to-be were inspired by spectacular weddings, such as those of Princess Elizabeth to Lieutenant Philip Mountbatten, in England, and of Grace Kelly to Prince Rainier, in Monaco. The formal, white dress began to move away from being a statement of high fashion to become more of a symbolic costume, designed to make every bride feel like a princess.

When John F Kennedy became president, he and his wife, Jackie, were regarded as America's golden couple. It was on 12 September 1953 that Senator John F Kennedy and Jacqueline Lee Bouvier exchanged wedding vows at St Mary's Church in Newport, Rhode Island. Here we see them emerging into the throng of 3,000 well-wishers. Designed by African American Ann Lowe, her gown had a 24-inch waist and was created from 50 yards of ivory silk taffeta.

⇽ star style

In 1954 Audrey Hepburn became the third wife of American actor and director Mel Ferrer. The antithesis of her curvaceous contemporaries Marilyn Monroe and Elizabeth Taylor, Hepburn chose clothes that accentuated her slenderness. Here she wears a full-skirted dress influenced by Christian Dior's opulent New Look.

⇽ good luck

In this informal snapshot both the bride and groom grip their horseshoes as if they were lifebuoys on the *Titanic*! The bridal gown is fashionable, in satin, with tight sleeves and a short veil, but it is the bridesmaids who steal the show in their swans' down-trimmed coats and muffs.

🌸 runaway bride

This couple eloped to marry in a church in Scotland in 1957. The photograph captures them looking happy but slightly tentative. The bride had bought her fashionable polka-dot, wide-skirted dress the previous year, but not as a wedding outfit, and she added the white ribbon trim for the occasion.

🌸 50s glamour

The formal wedding photograph reached new heights of glamour in the 1950s. This bride wears an extravagant dress and a train of chiffon, arranged to show its full glory. With sweetheart necklines and puffed sleeves, all the dresses are the height of 50s fashion.

↓ eyes right

The epitome of a stylish 1950s bride: wearing a modish, high-collared dress of lace over satin and a chic short veil, she holds a spray of carnations trimmed with motifs of lucky horseshoes and wedding bells. She is full of confidence – a quality that does not seem to be shared by her husband.

The Photographer

The earliest wedding photographers used the daguerreotype process, which required sitters to remain motionless in front of the camera for the exposure time of 20 to 30 minutes. Today, although we have grown used to seeing instant images on our digital cameras and mobile phones, the role of the professional wedding photographer has not diminished.

california dreaming

This thrifty bride has thought ahead in anticipation of showing off her dashing husband at smart evening soirées in her hometown of Bellflower, southern California. Her satin, strapless, full-skirted underdress will easily convert into a glamorous evening gown when the lace overdress is removed.

counting the cost

This service wedding is being witnessed somewhat disapprovingly by the bride's stern father in the back row. With ten bridesmaids and groomsmen, two flower girls, and a jungle of floral and palm frond arrangements, this father may be working out just how much the wedding is costing him.

shall we dance? ➜

It is Southern Rhodesia (now Zimbabwe) in the 1950s, when it was under British rule, and a stylish colonial wedding is taking place in Bulawayo. There is no hint of any African influence in this photograph; indeed, the couple dancing this first waltz at their reception could be anywhere in the world.

in deep water

Couples often say they feel breathless at the altar – and this couple had a better excuse than most. Reported in *Life Magazine* on 8 March 1954, this extraordinary marriage between American diving clown, Bob Smith, and 'aquamaid' Mary Beth Sanger took place underwater.

seeing double

A carefully posed photograph with the bride, glamorous in a satin gown with a long train, meeting the viewer's gaze only through her reflected image. Here we are allowed to witness the behind-the-scenes final adjustments to the veil by the chief bridesmaid who, unusually, is sporting a mini veil herself.

weddings with a swing

This image from the photographic chronicler Dr Otto Bettmann shows a double wedding in Harlem, New York. The bridesmaids and ushers have joined in the party atmosphere. The jitterbugger on the right seems to be drawing our attention to the flash of thigh seen through a slit in the bridesmaid's skirt.

85

כול חתן וקול כלה

← *mazel tov!*

A Jewish wedding, where the groom and bride's father both have something of the Cary Grant about them in their white tuxedos and slim bow ties. In Judaism it is traditional for the groom not to raise his bride's veil, but to place it over her face after the *ketubah*, or wedding contract, has been signed and before the public ceremony.

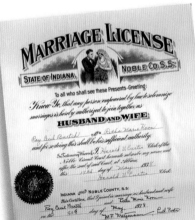

MARRIAGE LICENSE
STATE OF INDIANA, NOBLE CO. S.S.

To all who shall see these Presents–Greeting:

HUSBAND AND WIFE

Licences

Records of marriage licences exist from the 1520s in England, while it was not until 1923 that the USA established the Uniform Marriage and Marriage License Act. All over the world, intending couples must apply for a licence in order to legalize their union, and are charged up to £120 or $200 for the privilege, depending on which country they choose as the wedding venue. This rule also applies beyond our world. In July 2003 a licence was issued for a Russian cosmonaut and a woman from Clear Lake, Texas, who planned to marry while the groom was orbiting 240 miles above the earth.

cricket mad →

This wedding, in Bournemouth, England, with its batty guard of honour, may be the new wife's initiation into a cricketing marriage with weekends spent in the pavilion preparing teas. The Hampshire county cricket team did not win the County Championship until 1961, but no doubt this dutiful wife was present on that occasion to raise a congratulatory teacup.

← dizzy heights

This photograph was taken at the 1954 marriage of the conqueror of Mount Everest, Sir Edmund Hillary, and his bride, Louise. Edmund Hillary and sherpa Tenzing Norgay became international celebrities after making their heroic ascent the previous year. Here, Sir Edmund certainly looks more relaxed with all the media attention at his wedding than his new wife does.

just married...

Although a bride may yearn to be carried off by her groom on a white horse, it is usually the wedding car that fulfils this role today. Normally grand, occasionally quirky, the wedding car is where the happy couple show themselves to the outside world for the first time, so appearances are important.

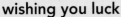

wishing you luck
Tying shoes to, or throwing them at, the bridal car, it is said, not only bestows good luck on the happy couple, it also symbolizes the bride's move from her parental home to the new one she will share with her husband.

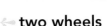

two wheels
A wildly impractical mode of transport for a bride in a long dress and veil, this unusual wedding conveyance was no doubt influenced by Marlon Brando's 1953 film *The Wild One*, in which a gang of 40 motorcyclists, the Black Rebels, gatecrashes a motorcycle race. Let's hope she didn't come to the same sorry end as Isadora Duncan!

↓ hollywood exit

Hollywood actress Jane Mansfield married Hungarian actor and Mr Universe Miklos 'Mickey' Hargitay in 1958. Mansfield first glimpsed him while rehearsing for Mae West's revue and, when asked by a waiter what she would like that evening, is said to have replied, 'I'll have a steak and the man on the left'!

happy indeed

The ceremony over, this beaming couple are on their way to the reception, pausing only for a photograph as they enter the special car, either a 'classic' or something grand like a Lincoln or a Cadillac. They will soon be sliding across that smart bench seat.

JUST MARRIED

CALIFORNIA
MAX 28

1960s

In the 1960s everything changed as Britain emerged from the shadows. Full employment and a dominant youth culture provoked a consumer explosion in a society now driven by the values of advertising and television. The American concept of built-in obsolescence was universally applied and the old traditions were thrown aside. Men's hair got longer while girls', along with their skirts, got shorter. Thanks to new methods of birth control, sexual freedom was widely enjoyed and many couples threw aside conventions by living together.

It was a decade driven by indulgence and popular culture. There were revolutions in music, art, architecture, design and fashion. Dress styles were radically changed by fashion icons such as Biba and Mary Quant, whose miniskirt became the symbol of the time. The style gurus were now musicians, actors, photographers and models. The American dominance of pop music was finally ended as hit records by British bands The Beatles and The Rolling Stones took the world by storm.

Towards the end of the decade the spirit of revolution became more powerful. In Europe students fought the establishment, while in the United States the big issues were race and Vietnam.

Despite the many pressures for change, the wedding survived, and thrived. Standards were set by the stars. Some, such as Elvis, took the conventional route, while others favoured a more bizarre approach. A notable example was the wedding between John Lennon and Yoko Ono, celebrated in Gibraltar on 29 March 1969. This famous image became a symbol for a radical decade that was, at its end, faced by even greater changes.

←three steps to heaven

This Dutch couple look relaxed and comfortable together, and perhaps are standing in front of the house they already share. Living together removed some of the traditional stresses and strains of the wedding day. Her dress is short, but high-necked, a blend of modernity and tradition echoed by the groom.

Confetti

Confetti originated as part of the pagan wedding ritual. After the marriage ceremony had taken place, the happy couple would be showered with grain, a well-known symbol of fertility, to wish them a fruitful union. The word 'confetti' comes from the same Italian word as confectionery and described the sugar-coated grain and nuts that were cast over Italian newly-weds.

⬅ please please me

Married in north London in the mid-1960s, this couple wore the high-street version of radical chic. Her hair, her dress, his narrow lapels and trousers say it all, though one wonders what her grandmother thought of it. Her strappy shoes give a mixed message of informality and elegance.

⬆ love me tender

King of rock 'n' roll, Elvis Presley first met Priscilla Beaulieu in 1959. Then only 14 years old, she was the daughter of an air force officer stationed in Germany, where Elvis was serving with the US armed forces. They married in Las Vegas on 1 May 1967, but it ended in 'Heartbreak Hotel' with divorce in 1973.

congratulations

The 1960s seem to have passed some members of this group by. The youngest bridesmaid gives a sense of period with her beehive hair, but it is only the older ladies who have noticed that skirts have got shorter. For everyone else, the classic look rules.

forever young ➛

This rather fearsome group of older relatives makes the point that modern fashions are best left to the young. Short skirts and dresses, modern hairstyles and strange hats, substantial handbags and unamused expressions give the group more than a hint of Monty Python.

↞ floating on high

Images from an American bridal magazine of 1966 show that there was more to the decade than short skirts. Perennially popular was this romantic look, with long dresses floating from a high bosom, echoing historical styles from the Tudor period to Jane Austen.

↞ top drawer

With her back-combed hair and lacy dress, this bride is straight from an early 1960s novel by John Braine or Alan Sillitoe. Her sharp-suited groom is also in period. Clutching the top layer of the wedding cake, she may already be thinking about the christening.

chapel of love

A wedding can be a wonderfully traditional occasion, unaffected by the whims and fancies of fashion. There is little of the 1960s in this timeless shot of a couple leaving the church and pausing before they walk beneath the arch of swords. A classic dress and a uniform tell the story, but her going-away dress was probably much shorter.

Telegrams

An essential part of wedding ritual, now sadly extinct, was the telegram from friends and relatives unable to attend. The reading of telegrams was one of the duties of the best man. Telegrams came in several styles and were normally delivered by the postboy on his bicycle. This example includes an unusual excuse for not attending the wedding. Apparently the sender was lost in the desert in Africa (but managed to find a telegraph office).

wanna hold your hand

Beneath the plume of her net veil, this bride is a true 1960s girl with a fashionable fringe. Her groom has achieved a perfect Beatles look, circa 1964 – even though this wedding was actually in 1968. They hold hands, tentatively cutting the cake.

teddy steady go

In the pre-Beatles era rock 'n' roll was king. Followers of Chuck Berry and Gene Vincent maintained the Teddy Boy styles well into the 1960s, as shown by the 1961 wedding of Pat and John Clark. Her dress is a tight-waisted, full-skirted extravaganza in lace, while everything about him shouts out the year – hair, collar style, tie. And his trousers had to be drainpipes.

1960s

baby love

This group with their frilly dresses bring together many 1960s styles and messages – Mary Poppins meets the Supremes, with a touch of Dusty Springfield. The page boy looks decidedly uncomfortable in his Lord Fauntleroy outfit.

dedicated followers

The attitudes and styles of the 1960s lived on through the decade. By 1969, when this wedding took place, flower power was all the rage but this couple are sticking resolutely to the classic 60s style. They look so informal, they might have dropped into the register office in their lunch hour. Only the confetti, the flowers and her lucky horseshoe give the game away.

← sign of the times

In the 60s the register office came into its own as many couples broke away from traditions. In church weddings, photos were taken after the ceremony, but now the actual moment of signing the register could be captured. This couple pose with the book in 1968, and her dress brings life to the plain, office-like setting.

↑ hippy day

This is a wonderful evocation of 60s styles. On the right a miniskirted, mid-1960s dolly stands beside her RAF husband, while on the left we have late-60s hippies, all long hair and long dresses. In the centre, looking traditional and timeless stand the happy couple.

a bride's guide...

Wedding magazines have become essential reading. Every aspect of the wedding is explored in the minutest detail. The Victorians were the first to produce bridal magazines, and every year more hit the stands. Full of inspiration and advice, they underline those old unchanging rules of wedding etiquette.

inspiration
When a girl decides to get married, her first stop is the news-stand. For guidance on everything from shoes to catering, the bridal magazine is a girl's best friend, and has been so for 100 years, as this 1920s example shows.

budget brides →
Traditionally the father of the bride picks up the tab, but today most families share the cost. Many magazines explain how to keep the show on the financial road.

MODERN BRIDE

AUG./SEPT. 75¢

EXCITING
FALL FASHIONS
photographed in
SAN FRANCISCO

HOW TO LEAD
A COLORFUL LIFE
INDOORS & OUT

MARRIAGE:
a paying proposition?

Honeymoons in
SAN FRANCISCO
VIRGINIA
THE POCONOS

Balene Selection

← **style file**
Last year's styles
simply will not do. In
the 1960s the long,
elegant look was
making a comeback,
easily keeping those
miniskirts at bay.

pretty as a picture
In addition to the numerous specialist bridal
magazines, a girl can turn to the big-name
magazines of fashion and society, which regularly have
features on weddings. The January 1962 issue of
Vanity Fair gives all those spring brides the
latest style news – which they
will ignore at their peril.

Vanity Fair

JANUARY 1962

16

Young Marrieds of 1962

Ubiquitous Jersey : Heavy Knits : Travel Clothes : Beauty

1970s and 80s

In the 1970s the Women's Liberation movement began to gain momentum, and the white wedding was seen as supporting the subservient position of the wife. Yet marriage remained as popular, numerically, as before. And the ease of obtaining divorces increased the number of second marriages.

Couples married at an older age, and women brought different expectations to their marriages. They were struggling for equality and the right to work and, in the USA, were active in their opposition to the war in Vietnam. The use of the birth-control pill meant they could choose whether or when to have children.

The early 1970s saw the young continue to reject the values of their parents, and this can be seen in novel wedding ceremonies and groovy gowns of Mexican design or Indian cotton. In the UK, Laura Ashley revived Victorian

styles and by the late 70s, with punk in full flood, it is a surprise to see brides in pinafores and full skirts.

As the world moved into depression in the early 1980s, wedding ceremonies returned to an old-fashioned expression of traditional values and, while women power-dressed for work, weddings became more opulent, and more formal.

The marriage of Lady Diana Spencer to HRH The Prince of Wales on 29 July 1981 was the quintessential 1980s wedding. Lady Diana's dress had to make a strong visual statement for television. The designers, David and Elizabeth Emanuel, decided to transform her into 'a fairytale princess'. The dress, of ivory silk taffeta with puffed sleeves, boned bodice, Carrickmacross lace panels, full skirts and a 6m (20ft) train, did just this.

victoria's secret

The influence of Victorian nostalgia and the products of Laura Ashley's shops can be seen in this wedding gown. It almost looks as if the bride is wearing a Victorian nightie over her dress with its flowing sleeves, pin-tucked bodice and short flounced overskirt. Hair is worn long and natural by both bride and groom.

afro style ➡

Michael Jackson and his chart-topping brothers were known in the 1970s for something they wore every day… the afro. They wore it to be fashionable, others used this hairstyle to indicate their support of the burgeoning Black Consciousness movement. This groom is a dedicated follower of fashion in his white wedding suit with wide, satin lapels.

←check this out

A group where the mini, midi and maxi hemlines of the day are all on display. The guest on the right makes the boldest style statement, in his flamboyant check jacket, while the guest on the left shows off her legs in a short skirt with a short haircut to match.

pretty maids all in a row

This could be a school outing, with 11 bridesmaids and flower girls posed on a flight of steps around the happy couple. The younger girls look charming in empire-line dresses, mob caps and muffs, made popular by the revival of interest in Kate Greenaway book illustrations.

daisy, daisy... →

Showing the ongoing influence of flower power, this 1973 bride wears a dress covered in daisy lace. Men's suit lapels were wide in the early 70s, and the bride's father, like many of his generation, has chosen a fashionable suit with matching waistcoat, rather than traditional morning dress.

↓ the empire strikes back

Wearing a high-waisted, empire-style satin wedding gown trimmed with lace, this 1974 bride is the height of fashion. She holds a bouquet of orange roses, symbolizing enthusiasm and desire. We can only hope her groom, dashing in a three-piece suit of air-force blue, lives up to her expectations.

⬅ fabulous flares

This could be a textbook guide to 1970s fashion. The bridesmaids wear trendy floppy hats to contrast with their pale or shocking pink outfits but it is the groom who steals the show. His dark suit with flared trousers is set off nicely by his black-and-white co-respondent shoes.

⬆ velvet underground

The unusual choice of a green velvet gown and aubergine suede suit by this 1971 bride and groom is a brave but fashionable choice compared to the more typical styles worn by their parents. But perhaps a creative side runs in the groom's family as the father wears desert boots with his formal wedding outfit.

107

Blow the Budget

Good form used to dictate that the wedding was paid for by the family of the bride or the bride herself. The groom paid for an engagement ring, a wedding present of a gem for his wife, his bachelor dinner and the marriage licence. He was also expected to provide buttonholes, ties and a personal gift for his best man and ushers, the bouquet and a wedding ring for the bride, and the clergyman's fee. Today, things are a little different, and the bride and groom often pay for the entire wedding themselves.

new romantics

Nostalgic sweetheart necklines, puffed sleeves and pastel pink give this 1980s bride and her maids a pretty, Victorian look. This was a time when weddings revelled in all the romance, the theatre and the grandeur that couples in the previous decade had regarded as 'square'.

← dressed to thrill

When the bride chooses not to wear white it doubtless takes a great deal of organization to ensure that the cake matches the gown. This bride has managed this costume and culinary double act, and has even persuaded her groom to enter into the spirit with his pink tie.

♪ soldier, soldier...

A return to traditional style with this military wedding: both groom and bride's father are with the Royal Artillery. The groom wears a frock coat and waist belt, while his father-in-law is decked out in 'No.1 Dress', complete with a dress sword trimmed with a sword knot of gold cord.

Stationery

Engraved black lettering on ivory or white card of a standard size was the particular style established in the early 20th century as de rigueur for wedding invitations, a style that had developed over decades in aristocratic circles in Britain. In America a professional calligrapher is often employed to address the invitation envelope, and a speedy response is encouraged by the inclusion of a reply card.

↑ a bed of roses

The bride wears a simple sheath dress beneath a confection of lace gathered at the neck and cuffs. This is an unusual design for the 80s, looking back to wedding dresses of the 1960s. The ribbon-trimmed bouquet is of pink roses which, in the language of flowers, means perfect happiness.

↞ magnum opus

The broad-shouldered look of women's street fashion in the 1980s has been softened and adapted in this wedding gown confection. The groom holds his new wife tentatively and has modelled his look on actor Tom Selleck's *Magnum, P.I.* – the laid-back, moustachioed private detective.

diana's double?

A dashing groom in uniform, a dazzling bride in ivory…at first glance this could be the 1981 wedding of Lady Diana Spencer and Prince Charles. Another look brings us back to reality: a windy day with a bride dressed in a copy of that famous dress. Although the design of the royal wedding dress had been Britain's best-kept secret, the first affordable replica was in the windows of a London department store in polyester satin just five hours after the wedding.

stage and screen...

There is nothing like a wedding to create a satisfying finale to any production, whether it is Shakespeare's *As You Like It* or a movie classic such as *High Society*. Audiences still enjoy the old theme of love gained, love lost and love regained, however it is revised and replayed.

star struck

Countless plays and musicals, from *Cinderella* on, have ended with a wedding. This 1906 postcard shows the moment when Miss Zena Dare marries Mr Seymour Hicks in *The Catch of the Season*. The writer of the card was not impressed: 'Saw this last week but was not struck with it. Similar to Cinderella but of course modern.'

dynasty drama

The 1980s soap *Dynasty* starred English actress, Joan Collins, as Alexis Carrington. Here she is celebrating her marriage to Farnsworth 'Dex' Dexter, played by Michael Nades. The show became known for its costumes, which boasted the biggest shoulder pads in television.

1789 A   MISS ZENA DARE & MR. SEYMOUR HICKS
(THE CATCH OF THE SEASON.)
ROTARY PHOTO. E.C

musical melodrama

Wedding in Paris was a romantic musical play of 1954, which followed the antics of Little Angy from Saskatchewan as she zigzagged her way through a minefield of men to cross the Atlantic and marry her childhood sweetheart in Paris. On the journey she discovers a lot about life and men outside Canada.

the color purple →

The screenplay of Alice Walker's influential book dealing with the life and trials of four African American women was directed by Steven Spielburg in 1985. In the film, Oprah Winfrey played the character Sofia, a large, fiercely independent woman who learned the hard way about the difficulties of combating cultural and institutional racism.

1990s and beyond

Divorce rates rise inexorably and in some countries single parents become the norm, yet the state of marriage lives on, the ultimate triumph of hope over experience. The celebrity marriage now sets the standard and everyone dances to the tune played by the stars of film and media, music and sport. Thanks to international magazines such as *Hello*, the world can be the uninvited guests at the latest celeb extravaganza.

Singer, dancer, actress and, in the view of many, the sexiest woman in the world, Jennifer Lopez married dancer and choreographer Cris Judd in the autumn of 2001. She had married before, in 1997, and had had other very public relationships but for her this was the real thing. At the time she said, 'Cris brings serenity to my world. In the midst of the crazy storm that is my life, his love is what I need most of all.' The wedding

was a traditional affair. This photograph shows Cris in formal dress and Jennifer wearing a lacy number by Valentino and carrying a big bouquet of white roses. Their famous wedding photograph is, as a result, relatively dateless. By the following June the marriage was over.

Despite everything, and all the pressures of the modern world, people continue to get married. There is still hope and celebration and the wedding photograph. For the stars, 'until it gets boring or something better comes along' may be the principle but for many 'till death us do part' still has real meaning.

And as for the style of the modern wedding, whether traditional or zany, it has echoes of that familiar song 'Anything Goes'.

↑ luscious landscape

An English summer landscape rolls away to infinity, a perfect setting for a very sophisticated and fashionable couple. He wears a flowery suit, she wears see-through lace and carries flowers that echo his suit. Here, as in many modern weddings, there is a sense of intimacy, with the photographer, and guests, intruding on private moments.

stepping out together →

Maybe this couple, in their shades and leaning on each other, and on the wall, for support, had their celebration the night before the wedding. Her biker boots may not have been everyone's first choice with the 30s-style dress and furry coat, but at least they match his leather trousers.

looking cool

This girl looks gorgeous, with masses of frothy lace, a big dress and veil, long white gloves, white pearls and a white bouquet. It is a traditional dress. By contrast, he is completely modern, cool and elegant in his blue suit. Together, they look great and are clearly delighted to have tied the knot.

marry me, marry my dog

The dog leads the way as husband and wife, organic farmers, resolute and cheerful, step out along the track and through an arch decorated with their vegetables. This is the country wedding, a popular modern type, with a hint of Arthurian England. The medieval theme is echoed by her dress, with its panels of soft red.

Shoe Style

Bridal shoes are often referred to as 'wedding slippers' and are regarded as lucky mascots. Tiny silvered versions sometimes adorn a traditional wedding cake. Arguably the most glamorous wedding shoes were those made by Clive Shilton for Lady Diana's wedding to the Prince of Wales in 1981. They were made of silk and embroidered with gold beads and sequins, and even the soles were decorated with a stylized floral design.

↑ and a subtle hint of raspberry

Tasting the wine is not usually a bridal duty but this girl seems keen to check the vintage, perhaps just to steady her nerves. This is going to be a white wedding whatever, full 1950s style dress, veil, long train, and the traditional bouquet of white lilies.

← on the dotted line

Register offices have never been busier, with more and more couples preferring a ceremony that is quick and informal. The real celebrations can then follow. This wedding, with its red-and-white theme, may be modern but the photograph is as formal as something taken a century ago.

↑ fairytale wedding

What could be more romantic than arriving at the church in a glass coach pulled by white horses? This radiant bride rests her hand affectionately on her father's arm, and her maids and footmen look on approvingly. Everyone is dressed to thrill – even the horses wear ostrich plumes.

a family album...

The wedding is the great family occasion that spans the generations, but it is rare to be able to tell the story of one family through four generations of wedding photographs, with the same people providing the link from one image to another. There is a great sense of continuity, and of the permanence of marriage.

setting the scene

Harry and Ada were married in Plymouth, England, on 6 October 1913. He was a milkman and she was a miner's daughter. Here is their typically Edwardian wedding photograph: a carefully posed group of people in their best, pictured, as usual, in the back garden, and all looking at the camera somewhat seriously.

the next generation

Harry and Ada appear in the next photograph, standing to the right of their daughter Doris at her marriage to Thomas on 25 September 1934. The relaxed and cheerful, but still formal, group is now indoors, in the photographer's studio, and the dress style is clearly 1930s, with slight echoes of Hollywood. Muffs and lacy hats are the theme for the bridesmaids.

swinging sixties

The pattern was repeated at Margaret's wedding to Tony, in Totnes, England on 12 March 1966, when her parents, Doris and Thomas, stood at her right for the photograph outside the church. It is a casual group, quickly assembled, and the equally casual and varied dress styles reflect their time. Notable are the long, simple dresses and the narrow lapels of the suits.

the modern way

With a wonderful sense of history, Tony and Margaret stand to the right of their daughter Julie at her marriage to Scott on 17 June 1995. Everything else has changed: the setting is the garden, the dress is a lavish creation with echoes of the Victorian era, and the men are in morning dress. This blend of formal and informal is typical of the late 20th century.

excited or what ⇢

The ceremony's over, now for the party. The days before the marriage can be stress-filled. Now she has said 'Yes', she can relax, enjoy her classically simple dress and let the excitement take hold. And she is still clutching that bridal bouquet, the flowers that say it all.

The Veil

A bride who wears an old veil, or even a borrowed one, will have good luck – an old saying that has led many a bride to wear her mother's, or even her grandmother's, wedding veil. Wearing a veil is an old custom, going back to the Romans. In Christian, Jewish, Muslim and Hindu cultures, it serves to ward off evil spirits and unwanted suitors, and is a sign of purity. Originally veils were worn from betrothal to the end of the wedding ceremony.

between you and me →

Today it is possible to get married almost anywhere. Illustrated here is a 'Love Ceremony', in which this couple pledged their troth before a high priestess in a field of wildflowers beneath a cloudless summer sky – by no means a conventional marriage, yet the bride and groom, a symphony in white, make it a timeless scene.

← up and over

It's a perfect throw, and the assembled hopefuls begin to jump and stretch, like rugby players tracking a high ball. Some are clearly keen to catch it, some not so sure, and some simply don't qualify yet. Even in a modern marriage, it is hard to beat the old traditions and those familiar rituals.

barefoot bliss →

Beach weddings are a romantic choice for couples wishing to escape from the constraints of traditional ceremonies. The beach chosen by this couple was accessible only by boat. The laid-back local registrar's only request was that he should be ensured dry feet on the day.

Speeches

'Darling, it isn't true', he seems to be saying. The speeches are the most agonizing, and sometimes the most entertaining, of wedding rituals. The father of the bride, the groom and the best man are traditionally the key players in a performance in which memory, fantasy, flattery, indiscretion and plain smut all seem to have a place. In the modern wedding, the mother of the bride, or even the bride herself may also say her piece.

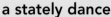 a stately dance

Three morning-suited gentlemen attend the bride and try to keep her, and her extravagant dress, out of the rain. She, veiled, clutches her bouquet, while her father looks after her train and the body of the dress. It is a scene, in subject and style, worthy of the artist Jack Vettriano.

windsor wedding →

After years of agony, despair, heart-searching and uncertainty, Prince Charles and Camilla Parker Bowles finally made it to the altar on 9 April 2005. In the event the ceremony, an eccentric mixture of the formal and the informal, and stamped overall with the complex personality of Charles, was a huge success. It was watched by millions on television, happy to share the romance and put aside the carping so beloved by the media. As she became the wife of the Prince of Wales and the Duchess of Cornwall, Camilla, dignified and delighted by the successful conclusion of a long and difficult courtship, won the battle of hearts and minds. Here, emerging from Windsor Town Hall, she wears a dress by Robinson Valentine and a hat by Philip Treacy. The celebrity marriage may be the marker for the 21st century but in the end nothing can beat a good old royal wedding.

about the authors

Paul Atterbury
Paul and Chrissie (left) were married in their Dorset village in June 2002. After a blessing in the church, the wedding party processed through the village to their garden, where a wedding tea was served to the accompaniment of the local brass band. Paul appears regularly as an expert on the BBC's *Antiques Roadshow*, and writes and lectures on a wide range of topics.

Hilary Kay
Hilary and Michael (right) were married in the British Virgin Islands in 2001. As keen sailors, they found the idea of a ceremony on a beach accessible only by boat very appealing. The wedding party comprised just the bride and groom, the registrar and two random witnesses. Hilary, a former auctioneer with Sotheby's, has been an expert on the BBC's *Antiques Roadshow* since 1979.

picture acknowledgments

The photographs used in this book have come from many sources and acknowledgment has been made whenever possible. However, many images inevitably remain anonymous, despite attempts at tracing or identifying their origin. If photographs or images have been used without due credit or acknowledgment, through no fault of our own, apologies are offered. If you believe this is the case, please let us know as we would like to give full credit in any future edition.

p10 The Royal Archives © HM Queen Elizabeth II

p9 © Tom Manley, Camera Press, London; p33 left, p110 top right Robert Opie; p22, p66 © Hulton-Deutsch Collection/Corbis; p42, p53, p78, p80 top, p85, p88 left, p89 bottom, p93, p102, p112 right © Bettmann/Corbis; p58 bottom © Rykoff Collection/Corbis; p114 © Reuters/Corbis; p123 © Stephen Hird/Reuters/Corbis; p50 top right, p76 far left © Nicholas James; p64 right The Museum of Costume, Bath and North East Somerset Council; p84 bottom left, p86 right © ITN Archive/Stills.

The authors and publishers would like to extend their thanks to all those individuals whose images appear anonymously in this book. We are also grateful to those who have generously lent photographs to be reproduced, including: Polly and James Amato, Paul and Chrissie Atterbury, Peter Barfoot and Jane Burden, Maureen and Terry Batkin, Richard Dennis, Michael Dunning, Mr and Mrs S Dunning, Mike and Liz Elliott, Sue Gordon, Edward and Elise Grace, Margaret Harris, Charlotte Hogg, Mark Kelly and Angie Moxham, Kevin and Heather Merrett, Adam Pressman and Ame Verso, Cerys and Toby Purser, Prudence and David Rogers, and particularly Doreen Smith at Frampton Weddings and Patricia Tanner at Weddings Past and Present www.weddingspastandpresent.co.uk.